You Too Can Create

STUNNING

Watermelon Carvings

How to Create Masterpieces from Watermelons

Jay Ball

Section One
Introduction to Watermelon Carving

Why Watermelons?

What do Halloween Pumpkin carving addicts do to curb their need for creative expression in July? They turns to watermelons, of course.

Where pumpkins can only be found in the fall season, watermelons are pretty much available year round. Yes, in many areas during winter months you may have to search harder for them and they will be more expensive when you find them, but they are usually still available.

Watermelon carving is becoming an increasingly more popular craft during summer months. You see creative watermelon art popping up at parties and other events more frequently. What was once a simple summer party snack is now becoming an elegant dinner event centerpiece. Creative watermelon carving has been featured in prestigious events, elite conventions and elegant weddings.

Now that you have this book, you can feature a work of watermelon art at *your* next party or event.

A Word About Temporary Art

My object in creating a beautifully carved watermelon is to create a special memorable moment. I like it when people not only enjoy my art, but remember it for a long time.

One great thing about ephemeral art (that means art that is short-lived or fleeting), is that it supports living in harmony with nature. Seasons change, leaves turn color, flowers bloom and wither. Life is always in a state of transition. Like Japanese sand and rock gardens, sand painting, ice sculpting, or sidewalk paintings, the art is on display only for a fleeting moment in time.

You may not want to see your child leave for their first day of school, or see them get married and move away from home, but there's no way to stop it. Life goes on, flow with it. Create something beautiful, then let it go. Then create something beautiful again. Don't try to stop the river, move with it. Live life to it's fullest, enjoy, then repeat.

On a more practical note, watermelons are biodegradable. You don't have to store them in your closet all year only to bring them out once for a short holiday season. It's sort of like disposable dishes. When you're done with them, you just throw them away.

Another bonus about watermelon carving, at least for me, is the joy creating a new work of art for each new season or event.

Finally, the temporary nature of a carved watermelon demands attention now, while it lasts. This makes them great attention grabbers and wonderful memory makers.

For Beginners and Experts Alike

How much can be written about a simple subject like watermelon carving? After all, it's quite simple really – just transfer a pattern, then cut it out – right? When you get right down to it, that's exactly right. Watermelon carving is simple, and I make no attempt to complicate it in this book.

With the growing interest in watermelon carving, more people are looking for information on the subject. Those new to it want to know how to get started. Those familiar with it want to learn more shortcuts and techniques for doing it better and quicker. In this book I have assumed the reader has no previous experience with watermelon carving. Beginners as well as those with experience will benefit from all the tips, tricks, and techniques I have included in these pages.

The temporary nature of a carved watermelon demands attention while it lasts.

Carving for Profit?

Watermelon carving is not just for fun either. Many carve watermelons for profit as well. Those trained in the art of creative fruit and vegetable carving can command $80, $100, $130 or more per centerpiece display. You may be cultivating a talent that is rewarding in more ways than one.

There's More Than One Way to Skin a Melon

There are a variety of books and videos on methods and styles of fruit and vegetable sculpting available on the market.

My style of watermelon carving lends itself well to the beginner, where you are guided by a pattern and it is more structured and easy to follow. The method I show you in this book will set you apart from most, but in the world of food garnishing, this is just one style among many.

The more advanced and free-form methods are in the area of Thai style carving, called kae-sa-lak in Thai.

While I do well with the form of watermelon carving that I show in this book, for the more advanced styles of fruit and vegetable sculpting I recommend the following great resources:

DVD by Chef Ray Duey, C.E.C.:
Fruit and Vegetable Sculpting
available at www.chefgarnish.com

The Complete Step-by Step Vegetable and Fruit Carving book,
hardcover 190 pages, edited by Nidda Hongwiwat, published by
Sangdad Publishing, Thailand. ISBN 9747162601

Advanced 3D styles of fruit and vegetable sculpting include Thai style carving.

Photo courtesy of www.chefgarnish.com, copyright 2005 Ray L. Duey, C.E.C., used with permission.

Watermelon Carving - In Three Easy Steps

In this book I reveal my own method of watermelon carving. This method involves the following three steps.

- Hollow Out the Melon
- Transfer the Pattern
- Carve the Design

(I told you it was easy.)

Are you ready to get started?

Section Two

Hollow Out the Watermelon

You will need to hollow out the watermelon when you want to light it from inside. If you do not plan to light your watermelon, skip this section.

Most of the patterns in this book can be used cut all the way thru or sculpted (where the outer skin only is removed). More on this in Section Three.

Adding a light to the melon (whether it is cut all the way thru or sculpted), adds an element of flair to your final display. I recommend it.

Typically, cutting the pattern all the way thru is easier, and this will *require* the melon be lit in order to see the design as intended.

Pick Your Watermelon

How do you pick a perfect watermelon for carving?

If the watermelon is perfect for eating, it's also perfect for carving. How do you know if a watermelon is ripe? Janet Ford of **www.DietPower.com** gives the following advice from an article entitled, "New Miracle Drug: Watermelon".

Is That Melon Ripe? The Straight Dope

Most experts agree: start with the color of the rind. It should be a dull green, depending on the variety -- but more importantly, the side that has lain on the ground during ripening should be creamy yellow. If it's white, it's not ripe.

Another major clue is the vine. If a stem is still attached, it should be brown. If it's green, put the melon back.

Its density should also give it away. "You should pick it up and say, 'Oh, that's heavier than I thought it should be,'" says Dana Abercrombie, director of the California-Arizona Watermelon Association. Heaviness means the melon has absorbed a goodly amount of water.

Kicking the Tires

There is no consensus about the "thump" test. Abercrombie recommends slapping with the palm of your hand, not your knuckle. "You should hear a hollow, reverberating sound, like in a basketball." If the melon pings, it's not ripe, she says.

Many people swear by the acoustic method, but others say it's like kicking the tires on a car. "It makes you feel good when you do it, but you don't know what it will accomplish," says Warren Roberts, a watermelon expert and an associate professor of horticulture at Oklahoma State University. Only an experienced ear can tell the difference, he says.

"A lot of people talk about that, but they can't really tell you what they're listening for," says Samantha Winters, a spokeswoman for the National Watermelon Promotion Board. If you're not sure, you can always ask the grocer to cut it for you.

Once you have the melon home, it will keep at room temperature for two to three weeks. After you've cut into it, however, it needs to go in the fridge. Or you can take care of it the way Roberts does. "I like to cut it open, eat the heart out, and then go on to another melon."

Tools

To hollow out your melon, gather the following items:

Saw. Since I have children I have a few safety pumpkin carving saws on hand and they work great for cutting an opening in the melon. A serrated steak knife or even a keyhole saw will work as well.

Parisian scoop. These are sometimes called mellon ballers. Even an ice cream scoop could work. The idea is to use something that will create appetizing morsels fit for eating. You could just scoop it all out into a big heap with a big spoon, but who would want to eat that?

Pumpkin scoop - scraping tool. I have found that the scoop that comes with the kits sold by Pumpkin Masters® during the Halloween season works perfectly for scraping (visit *www.pumpkinmasters.com* for more information on their tools). You will use this for the final cleaning and scraping of the inside of the watermelon.

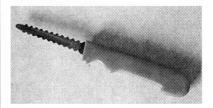

Safety Pumpkin Carving Knife

Parisian Scoop

Pumpkin Masters® Scraper Scoop™

Attach Pattern to Watermelon

Tape the pattern to the surface of the melon using transparent tape. Keep in mind that you have a flat sheet of paper and a round surface. It will help to cut slits in the pattern around the edges (see picture at right) to help it conform to the shape of the melon.

Adding slits helps the pattern conform to the round shape of the melon.

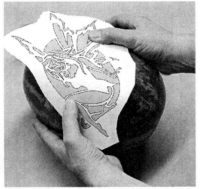

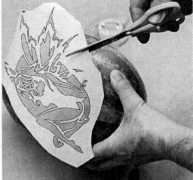

Pattern taped and ready to transfer to melon by poking.

Poke Holes to Transfer Pattern

Use anything sharp to poke holes thru the paper into the surface of the melon. Poke a hole every 1/8" (3 mm) or so, farther apart on larger areas and closer together in more detailed areas. When you are finished, remove and save the pattern. You will use it for reference when carving your design.

There are a variety of tools available that can be used for poking. Use smaller tools in detailed areas.

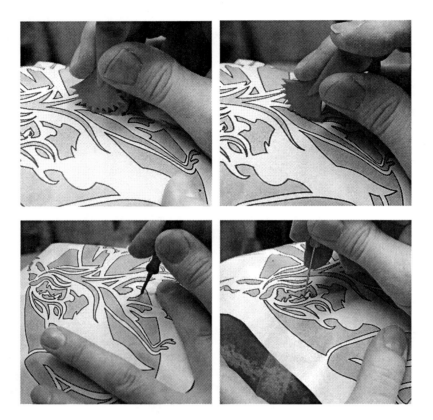

Stunning Watermelons

Add Powder for Clarity

You will notice, at this point, that the pattern is difficult to see. Take some white flour and pounce into the holes in your transferred pattern. Wipe the surface free from any remaining powder and you will be able to see your transferred pattern clearly.

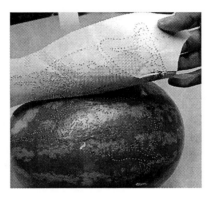

Pattern transferred and ready to carve.

Transfer Paper Method

Have you ever signed your name to a document and was told to "press hard" so that a copy would transfer through all sheets? How about carbon copy checks, have you ever used those?

In today's modern world, carbon copies are becoming more a thing of the past, but in the watermelon carving world, this could be the wave of the future. Once you've tried transferring patterns using this method, you may decide never to go back to any other way.

Tools:

 Transfer Paper. I've used fabric transfer paper that is available in craft stores (shown in picture at right), and it works well. Because the sheets are narrow, you may have to use two to cover the width of the pattern. I prefer the Saral® brand "wax free" transfer paper (pictured at left), available online at *DickBlick.com*. It's wider, and comes in a roll.

 Tape. You will use this to attach the pattern to the surface of the melon.

 Scissors. For cutting the pattern.

 Ball Point Pen. Get a smooth rolling ball point pen for copying over and transferring the pattern.

Tools required for the transfer paper method.

Transfer Paper Method Pros and Cons

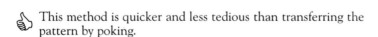 This method is quicker and less tedious than transferring the pattern by poking.

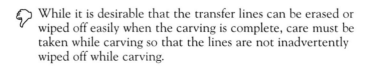 While it is desirable that the transfer lines can be erased or wiped off easily when the carving is complete, care must be taken while carving so that the lines are not inadvertently wiped off while carving.

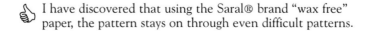 I have discovered that using the Saral® brand "wax free" paper, the pattern stays on through even difficult patterns.

Attach Pattern to Watermelon

Tape the pattern to the surface of the melon similar to how it was shown using the poking method, only this time add a layer of transfer paper between the pattern and the melon. Use transparent tape, and make sure the color side of the transfer paper is against the surface of the melon. As shown in the poking method, it may help to cut slits in the pattern around the edges to help it conform to the shape of the melon.

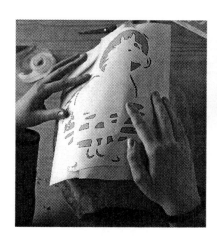

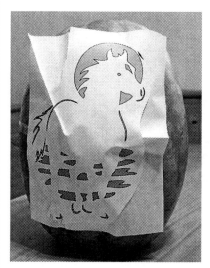

Pattern and transfer paper taped into place on melon.

Trace Over Pattern with Pen

Follow along the outline of the pattern with a pen. A ball point pen with colored ink (other than black) works best as you can better see where you've already traced. If the pattern includes hatching, outline these areas as well.

Once you have outlined the entire design, remove the pattern. At this point on more complex patterns, you may want to retrace over the transfer lines with a permanent ink marker to avoid them being wiped away while carving.

You are now ready to start carving.

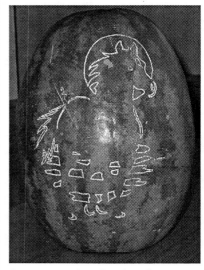

Pattern transferred and ready to carve.

Glue Method

Think outside the box. What if you didn't transfer the pattern at all? How about you just glue it on, then cut it out, pattern and all?

That's right. Follow along, I'll show you how.

Tools

White Craft Glue. Any name brand white craft or school glue will do.

Scissors. For cutting the pattern.

A Damp Rag. Have one on hand for easy clean up.

Tools required for the glue method.

Glue Method Pros and Cons

Pro. Quicker and less tedious than poking. No tracing or transferring of the pattern is required. Pattern is very easy to follow while carving.

Con. Can get messy. Have to wait for the glue to dry before carving (about 10 minutes with blow dryer). Can be tricky to carve delicate or detailed areas. When the paper gets wet it will begin to tear away and you can lose parts of the pattern.

Glue Pattern to Melon

Cut excess paper from borders of pattern. Turn over and pour glue onto back of pattern. You will want enough glue to cover the entire surface of the back of the pattern. Spread evenly.

Apply pattern to watermelon while it is still wet. Pinch and form pattern until it conforms to the surface of the melon.

At this point, either allow pattern to dry, or, if you're impatient (like me), you can use a blow dryer to speed up the process. Believe it or not, using the blow dryer can have the pattern dry and ready to carve in about 5 or 10 minutes.

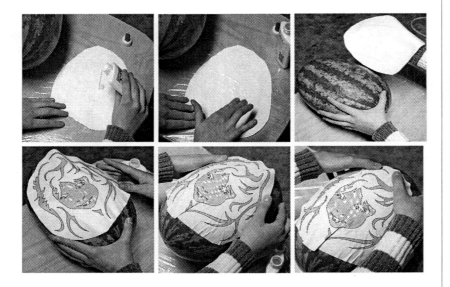

Blow dry to speed up drying time.

Pattern glued and ready to carve.

Wood and Tile Carving Tools. A simple inexpensive wood carving set has been very useful in sculpting. I also like the Speedball brand tile cutting set. In addition, Pumpkin Masters® also carries their own set of sculpting tools.

 Dremel® & Accessories. This handy little power tool is great for sculpting out large areas in a hurry. I go into more detail on using this tool later in this section. Two handy accessories for the dremel have proven quite indispensible to me for many projects, when carving either pumpkins or watermelons. Shown below are the Dremel® with the flex shaft (left) and the speed chuck (right).

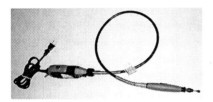

 Food Industry Garnishing Tools. If you are a chef or are into the culinary arts, you probably have a variety of tools that will work great for sculpting and carving fruits and vegetables.

An inexpensive wood carving set has been a great addition to my pumpkin carving tool box.

A good tile cutting set works well for sculpting in detail areas.

Food garnishing tools are designed for cutting fruits and vegetables.

Carved Designs

Cutting the pattern straight thru is usually considered the easiest method of carving. However, do not be misled by this. Some very intricate designs can be created this way, and they are far from "simple". Likewise, patterns that require some sculpting are not always "difficult".

Before you start hacking away at your transferred pattern, pause for a moment and consider your approach. Keep the following rules in mind as you carve:

1. Cut smaller details before larger ones.

2. Cut inside details before cutting outside details. Imagine cutting out the letter "C". If you cut the outer portion of the "C" first, you will discover that there is little support for the inside portion of your "C". The now weakened portion will increase the tendency to break off from the sawing motion, thus ruining your creation.

Cut inside portion of shape first

3. Work from the inside of the design outward. I've also had success with working from top to bottom, or from one side to the other.

4. Saw in a continuous up-and-down motion. Stop and remove the knife when you come to sharp corners and restart your cut going the other direction.

5. In delicate areas you may find it helpful to support the back surface of the melon with your finger while sawing. Watch out for your finger with the blade when using this technique.

At sharp corners, stop, remove blade, and re-insert going in the other direction. Don't attempt to twist the blade around sharp corners.

Cut out small details before larger ones. Cut out inside details before outside ones.

Completed carved "straight thru" design.

Section Five
Lighting, Photographing, & Fixing Mistakes

Like stained glass windows and most good people you know, your newly created carved masterpiece's true beauty is revealed when it is lit from within.

In this section I will show how to:

- light your carved melon

- photograph it

- preserve it so it will last longer

- correct mistakes

Lighting

I like to use a simple night light with a 6 ft extension cord. These are quite inexpensive and available at most department stores. Simply cut a slot in the edge of your opening, and slide the cord with the light attached into the slot, as shown at right.

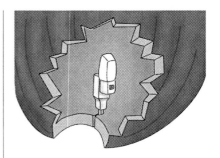

Insert cord and light into slot in watermelon to make your masterpiece glow.

Other Lighting Ideas

- There are a variety of battery operated pumpkin lights available on the market as well. Check them out at your local department store during the Halloween season.

- A candle can give a flickering glow to your carved melon and set an intimate tone to the display.

- Sometimes you may simply want more light. I like to light mine with 15 or 25 watts. I have designed a simple light stand for displaying my carved pumpkins and watermelons. You can download instructions for making this stand from *www.pumpkinglow.com*.

- Another light stand that I recommend for those who are serious about an even more impressive display is the one used by Chef Ray Duey. The stand he uses, and sells, is mounted on a turntable that slowly rotates as the lights change colors. You can check it out online at *www.chefgarnish.com*.

Light can add fire to your artwork.

Instructions for making your own light stand can be downloaded from www.pumpkinglow.com

Level 3 Patterns
Advanced

Abraham Lincoln, US
President 95

Bride & Groom . . .97

Bride & Groom
Kiss 99

Washington &
Lincoln, US Presidents 101

George
Washington 103

Baby's Hand 105

Eagle 107

American Flag
in Star 109

Fairy 111

Tree of Life 113

Level 1
Easy

Full Sculpt Option

Fireworks

Do not cut all the way thru on hatched areas

49

Level 1
Easy

Full Sculpt Option

Note: For more Valentine patterns, and great ideas for displaying them, get Jay's book, "Valentine Melons". See *ValentineMelons.com*.

Heart and Rose

Do not cut all the way thru on hatched areas

Level 1
Easy

Full Sculpt Option

Canadian Flag

Do not cut all the way thru on hatched areas

Full Sculpt Option

Easter Bunny

Do not cut all the way thru on hatched areas

Level 1
Easy

Carve Straight Thru
Option

Full Sculpt Option

Horn of Plenty

Do not cut all the way thru on hatched areas

Level 1
Easy

Full Sculpt Option

Hanukkah

Do not cut all the way thru on hatched areas

Level 1
Easy

Full Sculpt Option

Kwanzaa

Do not cut all the way thru on hatched areas

65

Level 1
Easy

Full Sculpt Option

Happy Birthday

Do not cut all the way thru on hatched areas

Level 1
Easy

Full Sculpt Option

Do not cut all the way thru on hatched areas

Hula Dancer

Level 1
Easy

Full Sculpt Option

Graduation

Do not cut all the way thru on hatched areas

71

Level 1
Intermediate

Full Sculpt Option

Moonlight Stallion

Do not cut all the way thru on hatched areas

Level 2
Intermediate

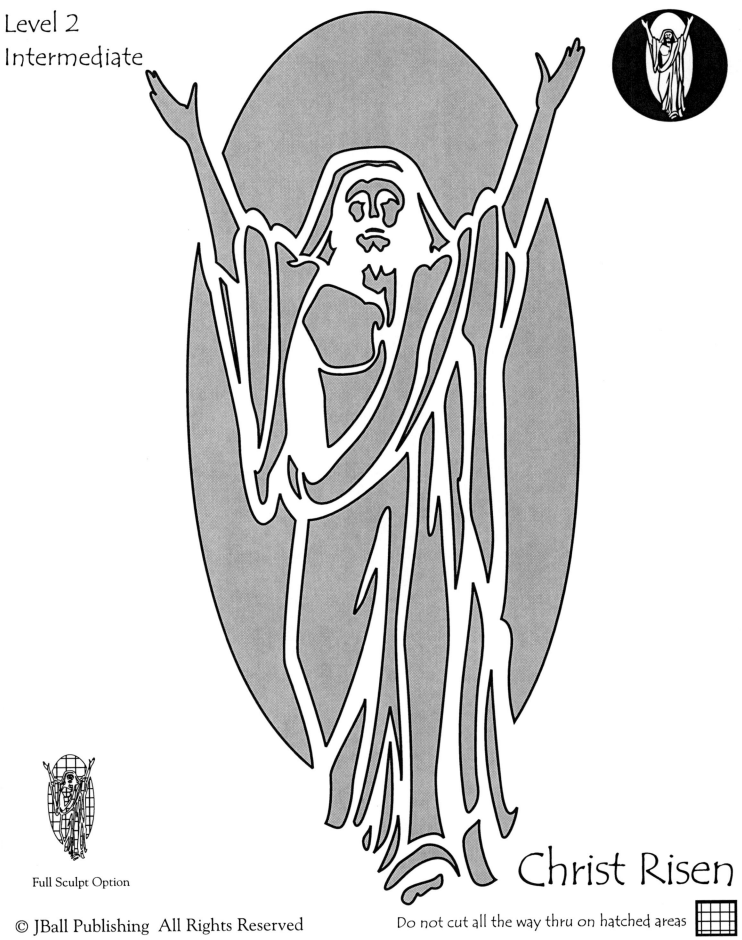

Full Sculpt Option

Christ Risen

Do not cut all the way thru on hatched areas

Level 2
Intermediate

Full Sculpt Option

Mother & Child

Do not cut all the way thru on hatched areas

Level 2
Intermediate

Full Sculpt Option

Moses

Do not cut all the way thru on hatched areas

85

Level 2
Intermediate

Full Sculpt Option

Santa

Do not cut all the way thru on hatched areas

Level 2
Intermediate

Full Sculpt Option

Tiki

Do not cut all the way thru on hatched areas

Level 2
Intermediate

Full Sculpt Option

Cougar Kitten

Do not cut all the way thru on hatched areas

Level 2
Intermediate

Full Sculpt Option

Do not cut all the way thru on hatched areas

Mountain Lion

Level 3
Advanced

Full Sculpt Option

Carve Straight Thru
Option

Bride & Groom Kiss

Do not cut all the way thru on hatched areas

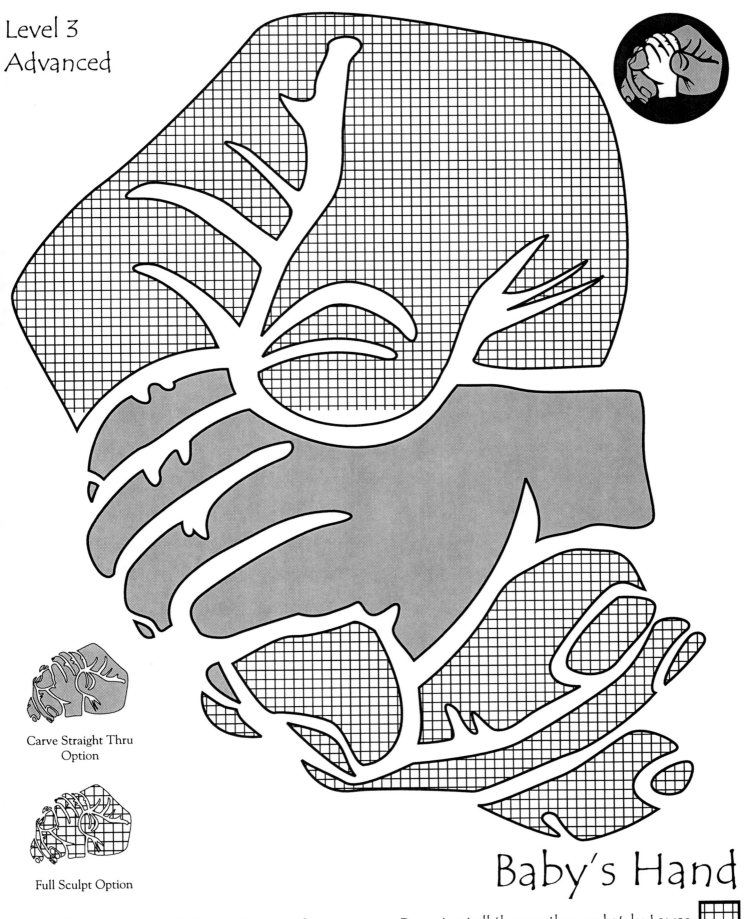

Level 3
Advanced

Carve Straight Thru
Option

Full Sculpt Option

Baby's Hand

Do not cut all the way thru on hatched areas

Level 3
Advanced

Full Sculpt Option

Eagle

Do not cut all the way thru on hatched areas

Level 3
Advanced

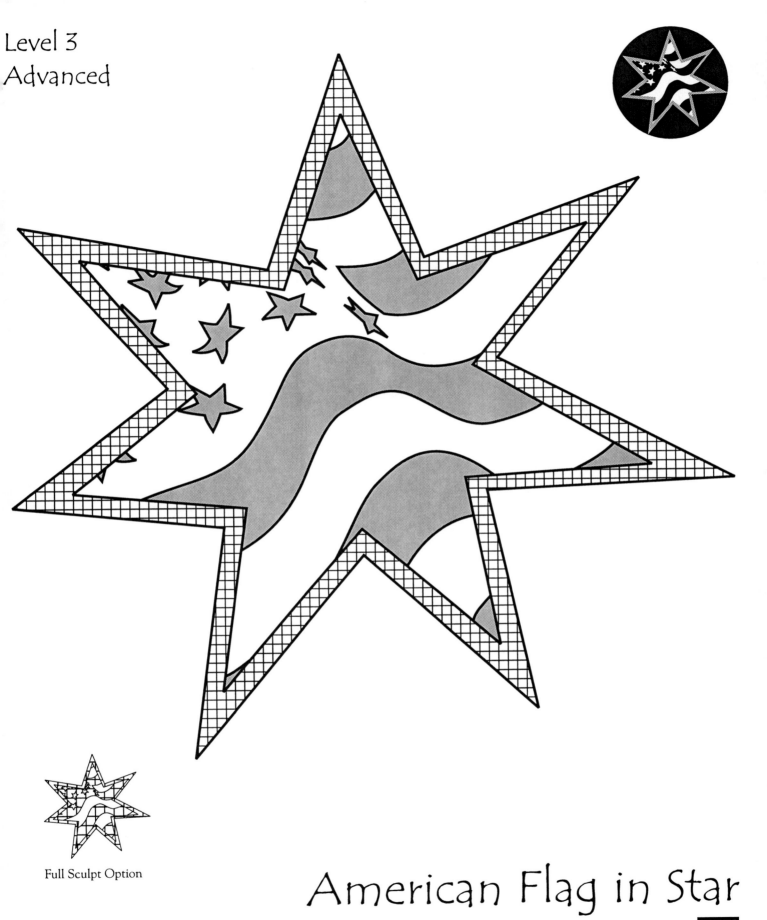

Full Sculpt Option

American Flag in Star

Do not cut all the way thru on hatched areas

Holiday Pattern Index
Chronological List of Holidays and Associated Patterns

New Years Day
Fireworks 49

Martin Luther King Jr. Day
Martin Luther King 75

Lincoln's Birthday
Abraham Lincoln 95

Valentine's Day
Heart & Rose 51
Bride & Groom 97
Bride & Groom Kiss 99
Daylilies 77

President's Day
Washington & Lincoln 101
American Flag in Star 109

Washington's Birthday
George Washington 103

St. Patrick's Day
Leprechaun 79

Easter Sunday
Christ Risen 81
Easter Bunny 55

Cinco de Mayo
Fireworks 49

Mother's Day
Mother & Child 83
Baby's Hand 105
Daylilies 77

Chronological List of Holidays and Associated Patterns – Cont.

Victoria Day (Canada)
    Canadian Flag 53

Memorial Day
    Daylilies 77
    Eagle 107
    American Flag in Star 109

Flag Day (US)
    American Flag in Star 109

Father's Day
    Baby's Hand 109
    Daylilies 77

Canada Day
    Canadian Flag 53

Independence Day (US)
    American Flag in Star 109
    Fireworks 49
    Eagle 107

Patriot Day (Sep 11th)
    American Flag in Star 109
    Eagle 107

Rosh Hashanah
    Moses 85

Yom Kippur
    Moses 85

Thanksgiving Day (Canada)
    Horn of Plenty 57

Halloween
    See Jay Ball's book on creating STUNNING pumpkin
    carvings. Also visit *www.zombiepumpkins.com.*

Chronological List of Holidays and Associated Patterns - Cont.

Veteran's Day
    American Flag in Star 109
    Eagle 107

Thanksgiving Day (US)
    Horn of Plenty 57

Hanukkah
    Hanukkah 59

Christmas
    Santa 87
    Reindeer 61
    Nativity 63

Kwanzaa
    Kwanzaa 65

Special Occasion
    Birthday - Happy Birthday .67
    Luau - Hula 69
    Luau - Tiki 89
    Graduation - Cap & Diploma 71

Other
    Fairy 111
    Cougar Kitten 91
    Mountain Lion 93
    Moonlight Stallion 73
    Tree of Life 113

Breinigsville, PA USA
19 May 2010
238282BV00003B/6/A

9 780976 417927